# PICTURES

## of

# Thoughts

ARTHUR JOHNSON

NEWMAN SPRINGS PUBLISHING
320 Broad Street
Red Bank, NJ 07701

First originally published by Newman Springs Publishing 2020

ISBN 978-1-63692-070-2 (Paperback)
ISBN 978-1-63692-071-9 (Digital)

Printed in the United States of America

January 6, 1997

## Prisoners

I watched a hawk circle high in
The sky; and my spirit filled
With the essence of time.
As I looked at the sea of mankind,
Where no bars or shackles could
Be found,
For everyone is a prisoner of some kind
I watched the hawk circle, graceful
And free, I wished a hawk, I could be,
For everyone a prisoner, don't you see,
Prisoners of drugs and of poverty.
Prisoners of greed and of false reality.
Prisoners of hate and of love.
If only they had the tranquility of a dove,
Prisoners of illness and of old age.
How it sets their hearts full of rage.
Prisoners of rules and regulations, manmade.
Prisoners of ignorance and of wisdom, they gave.
Prisoners of fear and of emotions enslaved.
As I watched the hawk circle high in the sky,
Flew a cemetery full of graves.
Prisoners of jobs and of work.
Prisoners of prisons, where many lurk.
Prisoners of pride and of lust.
Prisoners of lies that make a soul rust.
Prisoners of money and material things.
Not free like the hawk with golden wings.
For we're all prisoners of some kind.
Born of flesh and of mankind.
The only time we're not prisoners is when we're in the grave.
For God has set us free, by His son and the love He gave.

December 18, 1997

# The Emotions of Nature

The emotions of nature are vast,
That surrounds the conflicts of
Changes gone past.
The many faces and moods of the
Changing seasons, like a melody
That plays out and bears upon all things.
The wind that stalks the earth,
Like a giant that hounds the night and day.
Can be a friend or foe that
Laughingly plays with the trees,
Gently caressing its being like a
Gentle mother's hand, begins to
Turn violent.
A raging monster causing the plants
And all to tremble and shudder at
Its temperament, so dismayed,
Scars the earth upon which it moves
And returns to calm like a rowdy
Child, sulking at its destruction.
A personality of rain and snow and
Of heat and cold.
Nature has many emotions in which
Mortal man has little control.

December 23, 1997

## Poem for a Princess

Sorrow and grief covered the world
And walked among the mourners,
Like a darkening shadow that covered all.
And in its presence, you could
Almost hear the quietness of God.
As they stared solemnly quiet and
Forlorn.
By the millions, as the possession inched
Along.
Stood quiet, so forlorn in the midday-yellow
Glow of the sun.
As if the world and time stood still
Because of the sadness, so real,
Kinds and common people alike, stood quiet,
Their hearts torn by a passing friend,
A friend to everyone.
Stood unbelieving in the midday sun,
One of extended beauty and grace.
Who always tried to better the human race.
In the loneliness and solitude of death.
Comes a mass awakening.
Like a light that showed in a darkened
World amidst the ignorance and follies of
Man.
Still shines bright in the hearts of all.

December 27, 1997

## The Homeless

A person that has no purpose in life
Is like a cloud that never cries.
They spend their days and nights
Aimlessly drifting by,
Those who sleep on heating grates and in
Parking lot ramps.
Some people call them the beggars,
And some just call them tramps.
You can see them every day passing their
Life away.
Floating along without a song.
These folks without a home.
Did they just meet with mountable odds
In life, or are they happy in their own way.
The saddest part is of broken hearts,
These folks without a home.
You know a lot of the masters, bums of
Long ago.
Their voices were never heard, when
Living.
Until time took them out, now their works
Worth millions.
Homeless bums then, no doubt.

December 28, 1997

# *War*

Oh war, how long you stalk the hearts
Of men and scowl the face of God?
Rampaging upon the souls of man,
Can you hear the soldiers cry?
Man sitting on the edge of space, looking
Outward into all eternity begins to doubt
In spasms tomorrow minds will hod,
For on the verge of insanity one cannot
Be bold.
War, you beastly, ghastly thing.
How long you ravage this earth with
Sooty and blackened skies and dwell
Upon the hearts of those with peace
Still in their eyes?
Can't you hear the children cry?
War, how long you contend, ignorance to
Prevail.
Like a storm that has left the sail.
Do you hear the old men wail?
War, how long you growl upon this earth
And show your ugly face to the newborn
Babe that cries, who understands you
Not.
Don't you hear the women cry?
Oh war, how long must you cover the face of
God and mock his word to the lands of wod.
Do you hear God cry?

December 29, 1997

## The Lady

As I walked upon a summer's day
Hand-in-hand along the way
Wrapped in the arms of beauty, caressed
By her nudity
Her golden smile, breathtaking, as I
Caringly laughed and played.
Clothed with blue and green and colors
So arrayed.
This beautiful lady of tomorrow and
Today.
Swept me up to the mountains and into
The valley from which I lay and
Ruffled my hair with a breeze she sent
Along the way and warmed me with her
Smile that was beginning to fade away
As I walked upon a summer's day.
Beginning to get misty, shifty in her ways
I stopped and listened to the music she
Brings with her each and every day.
Hundreds of tiny instruments.
Striking tunes of innocence, how they
Played and played.
As the curtain of evening descended she
Slowly slipped away
Leaving me with memories, but will
Return tomorrow when the sun shows
Its way
Yes, I love this lady, a bright sunny summer's
Day.

December 31, 1997

## The Letter in the Trench

Oh lord, please stop this war.
I am over here across the sea.
The dead and wounded lay around as far
As one can see.
It's been raining every day and the mud
Up to my knees.
Oh lord, please stop this war before they
Kill me.
I hope to see my wife again and my
Family and be home soon so I can help
Decorate the tree.
But the bombs are bullets are coming fast,
It's as dark as it can be.
My three buddies just bought the farm
Well it could've been me.
Oh lord, won't somebody stop this war
Before they kill me.
We're killing each other over here and it
Doesn't make sense to me.
The sun is coming up, but you still can't
See.
For the smoke is as thick, as fog upon
The sea.
The shelling and noise have quieted down.
It's still as still can be.
Oh lord, please stop th—

January 3, 1998

# The Scarecrow

Tears of memories, of sweat and toil,
Slashed by the tattered scarecrow,
So all alone in the field.
As he looked down at the rusted, fruitless
Plow.
Stilled now by the tillers plight.
And into the yard of the old house where
Once joy and laughter flowed.
Gone, gone a long time ago,
And if you listened closely, you could almost
Here him whisper, quiet but low.
"I' am jobless now." He said as a crow lighted
Upon his brow. "Sold for taxes, land, and cows."
Stared, stared into the valley of weeds and
Brush below.
Stared into the valley of weeds, where
Once joy and laughter flowed.
"I' am jobless and useless now."
"Sold for taxes, land, and cows."

January 3, 1998

## A Cat's Meow

While sitting in the light late one night.
A mouse came out to browse and prowl.
Oh how he could hustle and tussle past,
Past my ashtray bustle.
Nothing meek, how he could squeak and run,
And run around.
I did my best to get rid of that pest,
But many a trap he disemboweled.
I couldn't have that, so I bought me a cat.
And what a cat's meow!
With shaggy hair, razor-sharp claws, and a
Killer's look in his eyes.
Twenty pounds of solid muscle, I could
Have bet on that mouse's demise.
Late one night I heard a ruckus.
He had him cornered behind a bucket.
Oh boy, we got you now
About that time, he let out a squeak and
Spit right in that big cat's eye,
And made a dash for his hole; how that
Mouse could dive.
I could've skinned that cat alive,
To call pest control cost me five-fifty-five.
But he was blinded in his right eye.
As for the cat he just lays around getting
Fat, and that's a cat's meow.

January 9, 1998

## City Streets

The city engulfed the old man's being
And held him prisoner, like a pack of wild
Dogs at bay.
As he walked in the bowels of the monster
With mumbling words to say.
As he limped along the lonely street.
Hostile and friendless, with his worldly
Possessions as he looked down at his feet.
Stopped and listened to the noisy street
And stared at the businessmen, dressed
So discreet.
A man tied to poverty and society's gaze
With no place to go, his hunger ablaze.
The smell from the vendors set his
Stomach arage, with no money at the
Ending day.
Began to look for a place in which to
Shelter and lay.
His body aching just surviving the day.
Watched him from a warm place
On that cold wintry day.
And feeling sorrow in my soul, gave
Him his stay
Thanked me for helping as I went
On my way.

# Chapters of Life

A person's life is something like
Chapters in a book.
Upon reading, of memories, we look.
First comes the newborn babe as helpless
As he can be.
That keeps you up most all the time.
You never are quite free, now!
We've come to chapter three,
Then we see a toddler, bouncing on daddy's knee,
Running around and into everything.
But it fills their parents' hearts with glee.
Next is the young man, a teenager we perceive.
Who knows everything about everything, but still
Lots of love in his parents' heart, wish
They would grow up and leave.
Then we see the middle-aged man.
With wife and family.
Working and scratching for his wife and four kids
And mother-in-law, Kimberley.
Next we see an old man and a retiree.
Living out his few years that's supposed to be
Carefree.
Until he meets the angel of death, well they
Always come to me.
Just another closing of a book and those who
Are left, memories.

January 11, 1998

## Stars

Diamonds in the sky are the stars
That shine.
Out on a clear night, right on time.
Sparkle and twinkle in hearts divine
Seemingly so close, yet so far away.
Wonders of mystery, leftovers from
The creator's hand.
Trillions and trillions, like grains of sand.
Scattered about on a canvas of blue,
How they shine, for me and you.
Wonders of mystery, like leftovers from
The maker's hand.
There is so many, like grains of sand.
Seemingly so close, yet so far away, scattered
About on a canvas of blue.
How they shine, with whiteish white and
Colors of hue.
Watchful eyes over me and you.

January 12, 1998

# A Joyous Moment

Death, some welcome it and some fear.
In final seconds when it is near,
Don't be afraid, there is nothing to fear.
A joyous moment where there's no years.
An end to suffering and the beginning of
Living.
To be with Jesus, so forgiving.
So death, who's afraid of you?
If you have Jesus, what can you do.
But to make this body disappear in the ground,
But will rise up when the trumpet sounds.
There are those who welcome you and those
Who fear, be it one or many years.
Only time you should fear a terrible,
Horrifying fear is when you look and Jesus
Is not near.
Then it's time to really fear, in the final
Seconds when you are near.
To live without Jesus where there are
No years.
The greatest wisdom I could ever give.
Is to love god, love one another with kindness,
For you don't know if He is near.

January 15, 1998

## *Love*

Love, the indirect purities of hate,
A word often used to attract a mate.
But for some, it's depleted at a rather
Fast rate.
For like a waterwheel, when the
Water is love, seems to lose its seemingly
Perpetual motion.
Love is like day and love is like night,
It makes one kill, it makes one fight,
Love is good and love is right.
But look what some sacrifice,
Love is sweet and love is nice
But for some it's cold as ice.
Some chance it like a gambler rolling
The dice and some hold on like a vise.
But most of all, love is the indirect
Purities of hate.
A word often used to attract and woo a mate.

January 15, 1998

## The Brook

How goes the giggling, laughing brook!
Through picturesque landscapes serene.
While butterflies play at her sides and
Snake doctors fan the weeds.
Laying down notes of music as she lazily
Went her way.
And wading across to the touch-me-nots;
Throwing out their seeds as they swayed.
You could feel the sense of beauty, never
Before arrayed.
Like a picture hinged upon the scales
Of time.
And minnows skipped across her brow, and
On insects dined.
Birds singing above her head with clouds
Looking down.
Some looked ferocious, and others looked like
Clowns.
Always giving and coming and blending
With the sounds.
A blessing of nature, where beauty
And tranquility abounds.

December 27, 1998

# The Old Crow

The old crow shook the ice and snow
From his being.
And cried out, as if to curse a cold and
Lonely world, and the wind and snow
Around him swirled.
Looking out from my window through
Icicles so clear and slender.
His echoes rebounding in the stillness,
Like the beginning of time.
A lonely sound, like bells that chime,
A lonely sound, like the beginning
Of time.
The demon wind howled through the
Cabin walls.
Like a pack of wolves at bay.
And as I looked through the cold and
Loneliness, the old crow became quiet
With nothing to say, his head bowled,
As if to pray.
Frozen solid, like a hunk of lead.
Stood like a statue against what I dread.
And with the setting sun the loneliness
And darkness crept into the room, with
Only the fire to fight its gloom.

January 25, 2000

# The Weeping

The tears that fell around me
Seems as hot as fire and it burnt
Into my memory, leaving a gigantic
Scar.
Mother Nature was crying for all her
Children that was going extinct.
Through the greed of mankind.
You better stop and think.
There was sadness all around me, you
Could smell it in the air.
Pollution from the factories and cars
You could see it everywhere,
The trees were scared and shaking,
Trembling from the ground.
Acid rain was falling and the leaves
Were turning brown.
The forests were dying, you couldn't
Hear a sound only the rustle of the
Dying trees.
There was no wildlife around.
The air had an acrid smell and the
Rivers stink.
If we keep up the way we're going
It's man who'll become extinct.

June 15, 2000

## The Clock

*Tick-tock* went the clock
Hanging above my kitchen door.
Keeping the moments of time
And nothing more, keeping time
It's daily chore, hanging above
My kitchen door.
Keeping time and nothing more.
Hear me tick and hear me chime,
Time is a friend of mine.
We have seen the rise and fall of
Great nations and men, whose
Legacies now hang in museums halls.
Where once forests stood, now
Shopping malls.
Said the clock above the door.
Keeping time and nothing more.
Keeping time; it's daily chore.
People try to kill and beat me,
But my friend has plenty galore.
Ticking away and nothing more.
Hanging above my kitchen door
Keeping time; it's daily chore.

July 5, 2000

## The Execution

You could feel the solitude as the
Angel of death stood near.
Some stood and stared with gasping breath
While others stood to cheer,
They led the poor black prisoner
From his cell, up the walk, through the
Door and up the stairs.
The murderer for the state stood and
Looked with a cold and icy stare.
Guilty or innocent, no one there
Seemed to care,
No calls from the governor, no stay
Was in the air.
They dragged him screaming and
Kicking and strapped him onto the
Gurney.
Injected him a lethal dose, his soul
Soon to journey.
"Abolish the death penalty," outside
The prison, they cried
"I'm innocent," the prisoner said,
As he drew his last sigh.
The state just murdered another poor
Man.
Who just wound up on the wrong side.

July 10, 2000

# The Funeral

Who is he? What is his name?
Nobody knows, that's why nobody came.
Only the undertaker and priest standing
In the rain.
No jets flew overhead, no twenty-one
Gun salute.
No big crowd a weeping, no crying out aloud
Only the birds a singing and overhead
The clouds.
The old priest was praying and the
Undertaker stood with head bowed.
"Take this unknown soul to heaven, God,"
He was saying out aloud.
For you know who he is lord, for we know
Nothing of his name, just an unknown
Soul lying in the rain.
Then there was a hush, a kind of mush as
The birds stopped their singing as if
To pay tribute to his soul.
Lying in his cardboard coffin, so still
And so cold.
For everyone is equal in death, it's the
Same, for great or small untold.

July 19, 2000

## *The Sunset*

How sets the setting sun?
With breathtaking colors when the
Day is gone.
With solitude and silence, like a
Fugitive on the run.
Painted by the master on a sky of blue.
Heavenly beauty for me and you.
That's how sets the setting sun.
Breathtaking colors when the day
Is gone.
Heavenly beauty for everyone.
Soon vanishes the day and darkness
Creeps in to chase the light away.
Left with the sounds of night.
How they echo and sway, but will
Come again tomorrow,
A brand-new day.
That's how sets the setting sun
With breathtaking colors for everyone.

July 24, 2000

# Just Another Day

The wolf howls for his time is near.
While the polar and grizzly bears show
No fear.
Where the antelope and deer used to
Play, is just another man-made
Development underway.
The birds sing a sad refrain, 'cause
The trees are dying from acid rain.
The eagle flies high above her aerie,
While the fish in the waters grow
Sick and weary.
The rich man laughs and the beggar
Begs, while nothing hatches from polluted eggs.
The elephant stares and hardly blinks
If we're not careful, we'll all be
Extinct.
Chalk it up to progress, that's what they
Say, the only thing that matters is
Profits and pay.
For the greedy and rich it's just another
Day, but in the end, we all will pay.

August 21, 2000

## The Passing

Bring me a rose that I might
Smell
The fragrance of heaven, not that
Of hell
Open my eyes so I can see, the beauty
Created for you and me.
Open my ears so I can hear.
The melodies and sounds of passing years.
Open my heart and let love abound.
Amidst a world where hate and evil
Is sound.
Open my mind to the wisdom of god.
Before they lay me under the sod.
Spare my soul and let it fly over the
Valleys, high in the sky.
Bring me a rose that I might smell.
The fragrance of heaven, not that
Of hell.

January 21, 2001

## The Butterfly

Life is like a butterfly.
Fragile as hell until you die,
Here today and gone tomorrow,
Floating along on hope, love, and sorrow,
Beautiful at first until you get tired
And old.
You realize the journey is over and
The grave is lonely and cold.
Just a moment in time I am told.
The battered and shredded wings
Of the butterfly tells its life story.
The battle of survival, not much of glory,
A thing of past beauty now ugly and
Scorned.
A little time in life, dies old and worned.
As it flutters and tries to flies,
Falls to the ground where it dies.
Swept away by the wind before your eyes.
Life is fragile, fragile as hell.

March 2, 2001

# The Little Blind Girl

The saddest thing I've ever seen
Was a little blind girl alone on
A swing,
She never laughed, nor did she smile.
Her heart seemed heavy for a little child,
"I've never seen the setting sun or
The stars that twinkle when day
Is done."
"It's always dark," she said to me,
"'Cause I am blind, I cannot see."
"I've never seen a bird in flight,
I hear them sing, oh, what a delight."
"I've never seen my mommy and daddy or
What they look like."
"I cannot run or ride my bike."
"If I had one wish, it would be to see
The light."
"I live in darkness, what a fright."
"I've never seen anything, only
When I sleep, only when I dream."
To me it was one of the saddest things
I've ever seen.

September 4, 2001

## A Thought

Once a time in autumn when crimson
Leaves were falling.
I sat perplexed, a thought I was
Deeply pondering.
A thought of reality, sadness, and of
Imaginative wondering; a thought of all
The earthly world.
As people sit and quarrel,
They say, "This world, with its frenzy
And blurtious turmoil,"
"If people get any smarter, they will
Eradicate their own self to the soil."
When their abode is empty with their
Thinking, in mind's marvelous confusion
And ecstasy, his place won't seem the
Same as before.
Ah! But once more as before, when material
Things are aglore will probe the universe
To find which is the score of everyday
Problems, as complexed as before.
Life, a mixture of sadness and joy, but not
To little children, say, a boy or a girl
Occupied with the past and present as
They laugh and play with their toys.
Find joys of being mothered and no doubt
Would have shuddered if they knew and
Understood the momentum of accomplishment
And glory.

September 4, 2001

## A Thought

They, when fully grown, set aside
Their laughter and play and go into
Majestic soleom nature way and go
Slowly and to each his or her own
Heart's way.
At the cross roads bent with decisions
Of daydreams and of visions in the
Future, his or her heart's way.
Then when they find their self and
What they seek, they are ready for the grave,
For it waits on no one.

May 9, 2002

# Sept. 11

The threads of time weave many
Scenes, some of good and evil schemes,
For events in time are unforeseen.
As the towers fell upon the sod and
Innocent souls made their way up
To God.
As people ran, cried, and screamed,
Like the devil himself was there
It seemed,
Came a unity as a nation that united
Us all.
As the world looked on with revengeful gall,
As the brave and courageous
Sacrificed their all.
From mountains and valleys to sandy
Shores, patriotism came out galore,
Thus united a nation and sent evil into
Condemnation.
Their love, courage, and kindness
Instilled in us hope, love, togetherness
And goodness for us all.
God bless the heroes that gave their
All.

May 10, 2006

## The Spirit

I was out walking, I felt
The spirit of God coming down.
It got so quiet as if the earth
Stopped turning around.
The birds stopped singing.
The wind dared not make a sound.
My eyes were opened, I could
See the devil walking up and
Down.
I could see he was planting his
Seeds of evil, with leaps and bounds.
Most people have 20-20 vision,
But a lot of them just might as
Well be blind.
Too much killings, too much hate
And greed.
That's the thing the devil nourishes
And he takes good care of those
Seeds.
But the reaper is coming, just
You wait and see.

May 14, 2006

## A Birthday

A birthday, just a place in time.
Soon passes like the echo of a
Bell or a song without rhyme.
A notch on the clog-wheel
That pulls one closer to the grave,
Where there are no sounds.
No matter how many, it's just
A moment in time,
Whether you have ninety, or you
Just have five,
It's all the same; a moment in
Time.
So lift your glass high, laugh, and
Sing.
'Cause this might be the last
Birthday that time will bring.

March 04, 2007

# The Mountains

The mountains stand like giants
In their coats of green.
The setting sun in the west
Is the prettiest mystery I've
Ever seen.
The birds that sing from dawn
To night make a harmonious
Sound, and if you listen late
At night, the whistle of a train
Coming around.
The whip-poor-wills that call at
Night make a lonely sound.
It always reminds me of you
When you were always around.
And if I look towards the
Sky at night, I see you as
A star smiling down.
The flowers by day show off their
Colors with pride, but some that
Grow deep in the forest, it seems
They're trying to hide.
From a world where no peace
And quiet abide.

June 4, 2008

## The Old Man

The old man
      On the bench sat with cane
      And hands a trembling
Who in his mind was remembering.
Days of his youth and love simmering
Long ago as a fading echo, like moonlight
On water glimmering.
Sat and spat into the dirt, by the
Vacuum in his eyes; I knew his body and
Soul did hurt.
Dozing off to the land of nod. Just to
Awaken with a shudder.
The sounds of his voice would flutter and
Stutter.
Went again to the land of nod and
Through the tunnel of light, never
To return no more.